Jamaica's Blue Marker

Juanita Havill   Illustrated by Anne Sibley O'Brien

HOUGHTON MIFFLIN COMPANY
BOSTON
ATLANTA   DALLAS   GENEVA, ILLINOIS   PALO ALTO   PRINCETON

For Linda Katz and Marcia Moon
of the Children's Literacy Initiative

—J.H.

For Emmett and all the Peaks Islanders who over
the years have loaned me their faces

—A. S. O'B

Jamaica's Blue Marker, by Juanita Havill, illustrated by Anne Sibley O'Brien. Text copyright © 1995 by Juanita Havill. Illustrations copyright © 1995 by Anne Sibley O'Brien. Reprinted by permission of Houghton Mifflin Company. All rights reserved.

2000 Impression
Houghton Mifflin Edition, 1997

No part of this work may be reproduced or transmitted in any form or by any means, electronic or mechanical, including photocopying and recording, or by any information storage or retrieval system, without the prior written permission of the copyright owner unless such copying is expressly permitted by federal copyright law. With the exception of nonprofit transcription in Braille, Houghton Mifflin is not authorized to grant permission for further uses of this work. Permission must be obtained from the individual copyright owner as identified herein.

Printed in the U.S.A.

ISBN: 0-395-81082-5

456789-B-02 01 00 99

Jamaica's Blue Marker

Jamaica closed her eyes and thought about her picture.
Mrs. Wirth always said to think first, then draw.

Jamaica opened her eyes and drew a tree on her big sheet of paper. Then she drew leaves falling off the tree and colored them yellow.

"Jamaica," Mrs. Wirth said, "could you please share your markers with Russell? He doesn't have any."

He never has anything he needs, Jamaica thought. But she said, "Okay," even though she didn't want to share her markers with him.

Russell brought his paper to Jamaica's table. He sat down beside her and grabbed her blue marker. Jamaica picked up her brown and orange markers to finish her picture. She didn't pay any attention to Russell. After a while she peeked at his paper. Russell was making squiggly circles all over his page.

"We're supposed to draw a fall picture, Russell," Jamaica said.

"Who says?"

"Mrs. Wirth. Don't you ever listen?"

"I don't have to." Russell reached out with the blue marker and made a streak across Jamaica's picture.

"Russell, stop!" Jamaica shouted.
But Russell scribbled all over Jamaica's yellow-leafed tree.

"Mrs. Wirth," Jamaica cried. "Russell wrecked my picture."

Mrs. Wirth hurried over to their table. "Russell, did you do this?" She held up Jamaica's picture.

Mrs. Wirth couldn't get Russell to say "I'm sorry." He had to go sit alone and work on spelling until art was over.

"Look what Russell did!" Jamaica showed her father and brother when she got home. "I tried, but I couldn't make another one as good as this." When she looked at the ugly blue squiggles, she had to swallow hard not to cry. "Russell is a mean brat."

"Did you tell Mrs. Wirth what happened?" her father asked.

Jamaica nodded. "Russell can't use my markers again. I shared with him because he didn't have any. He never has what he's supposed to have. But that's no reason to be mean."

"No," her father said. "Russell shouldn't have messed up your picture."

The next time they had art Jamaica was glad Russell didn't sit at her table. Then he couldn't bother her, and she didn't have to share her markers with him, either. But at recess Russell threw sand at her and chased two second-grade girls, so he had to go to the office.

Before he came back, Mrs. Wirth said, "I would like to tell you something. Can you keep a secret?"

"Yes!" Jamaica shouted with her classmates.

"We are going to have a going-away party for Russell on Friday. His father has a new job in another town. They will be moving over the weekend. I thought that you might like to make cards to say good-bye. Then Russell will have something to remember us by."

Mrs. Wirth passed out paper. Then she showed everyone how to fold the paper into a card. Jamaica didn't want to make a card for Russell. She was glad he was moving. Then he wouldn't bother her anymore. She put the paper in her desk.

At supper, Jamaica said, "I like living here. I like my house and my room and the tree in the front yard. I like my school, too."

"I'm glad you do," her mother said.

"I wouldn't like to move."

"Who said anything about moving?" Ossie asked.

"Russell is moving," Jamaica said.

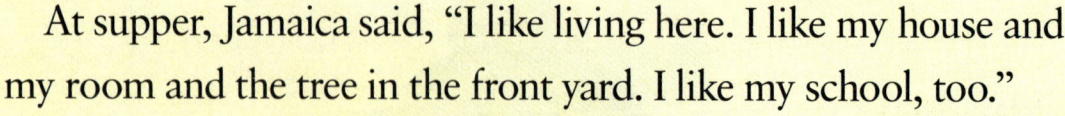

"Lucky you. He won't mess up your pictures anymore," Ossie said.

"I wonder how Russell feels about moving," Dad said. "He might be upset. Has he talked about it?"

"Russell doesn't say anything. He just gets in trouble," Jamaica said.

Russell didn't come to the classroom on Friday morning. He was with his mother in the office. Jamaica looked at his empty desk. Next week Russell would be gone. He wouldn't be at his desk ever again.

She decided to make a card for Russell. She got out the blank card and her markers, too.

But just then Mrs. Wirth asked, "Who are my helpers this week?" Jamaica raised her hand.

"Jamaica, could you collect the cards and put them in Russell's desk? Brianna and Thomas, I'd like for you to clear the activity table for the plates and cups."

Jamaica went from desk to desk to pick up the cards. She put the whole stack in Russell's desk. As she closed his desk, Russell came in with his mother.

The party started. They played games for a while and ate cake. Russell opened his desk and took out all the cards. "Look, Mom. Everybody made a card for me."

Not everybody, Jamaica thought. She took the blue marker out of her marker bag. Then she ran up to Russell.

"This is for you, Russell." She handed him the marker. "You can use it at your new school."

"But you might need it," he said. "You like to draw. You draw the best pictures in the class. What if you have to color the sky?"

"Someone will share with me."

"Thanks," he said. "You're lucky. You get to stay here."

Now Jamaica knew how Russell felt about moving. "I wish you didn't have to move," she said.

When Jamaica waved good-bye to Russell, she noticed that his mother was carrying his good-bye cards. Russell held up the blue marker and waved it at her as if he'd won a prize.

"Good-bye, Russell. I'll miss you," Jamaica said. And she meant it.